The impact of multinational enterprises
on employment and training

The impact of multinational enterprises on employment and training

International Labour Office — Geneva

ISBN 92-2-101478-9

First published 1976
Second impression 1977

Printed by Imprimeries Populaires, Geneva, Switzerland

TABLE OF CONTENTS

THE IMPACT OF MULTINATIONAL ENTERPRISES ON THE GROWTH OF EMPLOYMENT IN DEVELOPING COUNTRIES

Direct employment creation

In 1970 the number of jobs made available by multinational enterprises was estimated at 13 or 14 millions for all market economy countries.[1] Of these 13-14 million, a bare 2 million were created in developing countries.

In proportion to the total labour force of developing countries, this is obviously small - about 0.3 per cent - but compared to the number of unemployed persons looking for work (54 million in 1973[2]), this performance by the multinational enterprises is appreciable. Without their contribution unemployment would undoubtedly be higher.

Macro-economic comparisons of this kind mean little, however. The over-all contribution of foreign capital to capital formation in developing countries is very small; for example, in the period 1961-69, foreign private investment in Latin America accounted for not more than 4 or 5 per cent of total capital formation.[3] Moreover, foreign investments are not made in every developing country, but are very concentrated geographically.

Concentration of foreign private investment

(Development Assistance Committee Countries - 1972)

Region	Millions of US $ (total for the region)	Countries (per cent)	
Africa	9 404.0	Gabon Nigeria Libya Zaire	3.9 22.3 16.5 6.5
Asia	8 836.0	India Indonesia Malaysia	18.7 13.5 11.3
Middle East	3 941.0	Saudi Arabia Iran Kuwait	26.6 25.3 18.3
Latin America	2 583.0	Brazil Venezuela Argentina Mexico	23.8 14.3 8.9 10.2

Source: OECD: Stock of private investments by DAC countries in developing countries, end 1972, Paris, 1974.

---

[1] United Nations: Multinational corporations and world development, ST/ECA/10, New York, 1975.

[2] This estimate excludes underemployed workers.

[3] C.V. Vaitsos: "Employment effects of foreign direct investments in developing countries", Tecnología para el desarrollo, Mexico City, 1974.

For these two reasons a comprehensive approach to the volume of direct employment creation by multinational enterprises is of no value. The phenomenon has to be ascertained for each country separately. Even then, analysis of direct effects on employment is distorted by the fact that multinational investments are confined to a few industries. The situation is also radically different according to whether multinational enterprises in any given country are concerned with the extraction of raw materials, integration into an import substitution process, or the use of cheap labour:

1. Extraction of natural resources

This is traditionally the most usual relationship between foreign capital and developing countries.

In the extractive industries, production processes are highly capital intensive and the degree of capital intensiveness does not depend on the firm's nationality. National and foreign firms both have to adopt current production processes; in other words, there is at any given moment practically no choice of technology in these industries.

Technical progress in large raw material production units results in a higher capital-labour ratio (for example, in the big mining companies in Chile, the capital-labour ratio was 117,500 US $ in 1950 and 187,800 US $ in 1960[1]) and a parallel fall in the number of persons employed, as the following statistics show:

Country	Employment in extractive industries		
Chile (copper)	1943: 24 777 persons 1954: 14 320 "		
Venezuela (petroleum)	1950: 110 million man-hours 1964: 64 " " "		
Gabon (petroleum, manganese, uranium)	1960: 14 800 persons 1970: 8 400 "		
Malaysia (tin)	1965: 100 index (1970 = 100) 1973: 84.0 " " "		
Chile (all extractive industries)	1964: 140.6 " " " 1971: 98.0 " " "		

Sources: Vaitsos, op. cit; Yearbook of Labour Statistics, ILO, Geneva, 1974.

The fall in employment in the extractive industries is due not only to greater capital intensiveness, but also to the fact that many jobs in these industries are temporary ones linked to the installation of an initial infrastructure.

For example, the MIFERMA Company mining iron-ore deposits in Mauritania hired 3,800 Mauritanians to work on infrastructure projects and dismissed them once they were finished.[2] In Gabon, as has been seen, the number of wage earners in the mining sector fell from 14,800 in 1960 to 8,400 in 1970. This is explained by the large-scale operations carried out in the 1960s to create an infrastructure for the extraction of manganese and uranium.

---

[1] Vaitsos, op. cit.

[2] COGERAF, Monographie de 31 pays africains, Paris, 1964.

Even in countries in which employment did not fall, the considerable volume of investment in the extractive industries is out of all proportion to the direct labour employed. In Chile, Argentina, Brazil and Mexico, the proportion of employment in the "mining and petroleum" sector in 1960 was respectively 4.1, 0.6, 2.5 and 1.2 per cent.[1] In Jamaica, where the mining sector is dominated by multinational enterprises producing bauxite, employment in the extractive industries did not account for more than 0.5 per cent of the labour force, in spite of some increase between 1958 (2,600) and 1963 (3,600).[2]

The reasons why multinational enterprises in the mining sector have created so few jobs are essentially technical (a very high capital-labour ratio), and no enterprise, multinational or not, can evade them.

2. Promotion of import substitution in the industrial sector

This arises when foreign capital helps to develop industrial activities directed at the domestic market in developing countries, so altering the traditional pattern of these countries' integration into the world market. This began after the First World War and later led to the break-up of the multinational system of trade and payments and a considerable reduction of imports into industrialised countries. At that time, developing countries were obliged to look to their own interests and this almost automatically created conditions for protected industrial development and import substitution. When this process was partly accomplished, investments of foreign capital in developing countries began to increase enormously. Interest in certain types of investments in developing countries, principally in the manufacturing sector, developed as never before from the end of the Second World War onwards.

Year	Book value of total United States investments in Latin America (in millions of dollars)	Investment in manufacturing (per cent)
1940	2 500	8
1945	3 000	13
1950	4 735	17
1955	6 608	21
1960	8 139	25
1968	13 000	31

Sources: 1940-60, M. Ikonikoff: "Les investissements étrangers en Amérique Latine", in Revue tiers-monde (Paris), Oct.-Dec. 1970; 1968, ECLA: Estudio económico de América Latina, 1970, Vol. II, p. 10.

A spectacular increase in foreign capital began at the end of the 1950s. The rate of growth of capital invested in the manufacturing sector was 7 per cent in 1950 and 12.8 per cent from 1960 to 1968.[3] The following table provides a clear comparison of the dynamism of foreign capital and national capital respectively in the industrial growth of selected countries.

---

[1]
C.V. Vaitsos, op. cit.

[2]
N. Girvan, Foreign capital and economic underdevelopment in Jamaica, University of the West Indies, 1971.

[3]
ECLA, op. cit., p. 13.

Country	Annual rate of growth in sales of subsidiaries of multinational enterprises, 1961-65 (1)	Annual rate of growth of total national industrial production 1961-65 (2)	Ratio of (1) to (2)
Argentina	13.7	5.7	2.40
Brazil	4.7	2.0	2.35
Mexico	16.9	7.4	2.28
Venezuela	13.2	9.4	1.40
Philippines	11.8	5.9	2.00

Source: CEPAL, op. cit., p. 67.

These investments are not equally distributed over the developing world. Most of them go to the largest countries, the most important markets and the most developed processes. In 1968, the three largest countries in Latin America accounted for 74 per cent of the total investment in manufacturing in the American Continent.

In addition, a notable change has become apparent in the distribution of investment within manufacturing. The following figures show this:

Direct United States investment in manufacturing in Latin America

In millions of dollars

	1929	1936	1940	1950	1957	1963
Food products	122	78	62	158	200	300
Chemicals (including rubber)	24	29	76	265	467	736
Metal and engineering industries	49	46	37	197	382	808
Textiles, paper and other industries	36	57	35	160	230	366
Total:	230	210	210	780	1 280	2 210

Per cent

	1929	1936	1940	1950	1957	1963
Food products	53.0	37.0	30.0	20.0	15.5	13.5
Chemicals (including rubber)	10.5	14.0	36.0	34.0	36.5	33.5
Metal and engineering industries	21.0	22.0	17.5	25.5	30.0	36.5
Textiles, paper and other industries	15.0	27.0	16.5	20.5	18.0	16.5
Total:	100.0	100.0	100.0	100.0	100.0	100.0

Source: A. Dorfman: La industrialización en América Latina; Las políticas de fomento, Fondo de Cultura Económica, Mexico City, 1967, p. 210.

It will be seen that there is a positive relationship between foreign investment and dynamic growth in certain branches.

Lastly, in the import substitution process, multinational enterprises integrate themselves as far as possible into the local market in order to obtain a dominant position. The following data compiled by the Harvard Group are highly significant in this respect.

Geographical distribution of sales of multinational enterprises

Host country	Subsidiaries' main market			
	Firms of US origin (1971)		Others (1968)	
	Local market	Exports	Local market	Exports
North America	97.3	2.7	96.1	3.9
Latin America	97.1	2.9	93.3	6.7
Europe	92.4	7.6	91.5	8.5
Africa and Middle East	95.1	4.9	94.2	5.8
Rest of Asia and Oceania	91.0	9.0	90.6	9.4

Source: J.W. Vaupel, J.P. Curham; The world's multinational enterprises,
Centre d'études industrielles, Geneva, 1974, pp. 381-382.

This is not to say that multinational enterprises do not occupy a strategic
place in the exports of manufactured products from developing countries, but these
are mainly marginal activities determined by specific factors (certain limited
requirements imposed by host countries, surplus production capacity, development of
captive markets, gradual integration of countries bordering on privileged host
countries, etc.).

Multinational enterprises engaged in import substitution generally operate in
highly capital-intensive industries which do little for employment creation.

For all developing countries taken together, the number of persons (including
expatriates) employed by United States multinational enterprises was:

All developing countries. Employment in United States
multinational manufacturing enterprises
(in thousands of persons, 1966)

Sectors	Employment
Food products	100
Chemicals	110
Semi-finished products	42
Machinery	101
Transport equipment	45
Others	127
Total	525

Source: US Department of Commerce: US direct investment abroad, 1966 - Final
data, Washington, DC, 1975.

The number of persons employed by United States multinational manufacturing
enterprises is not enormous in absolute figures: it was 525,000 for the developing
countries in 1966, but as already pointed out, its distribution over those countries
was very unequal.

There was a sharp increase in employment in multinational manufacturing enterprises between 1966 and 1970 - an average of 8.3 per cent yearly[1] (more than the

---

[1] US Department of Commerce: Special survey of US multinational companies,
1970, 1972.

total growth in employment in the manufacturing sector during the same period) and about 4 per cent for all developing countries. The machinery and transport equipment sectors were particularly dynamic and accounted for the greatest increases in employment.

As a result of the large increase in labour productivity, sales by multinational enterprises increased much more than employment. This is true of all multinational enterprises, whether United States-based or not.

The impact of multinational enterprises on direct employment creation can only be correctly appreciated against the background of each country. There is a lack of information on this point and so far as this writer is aware, there are few statistics on employment in the manufacturing sector giving a breakdown of the firms concerned by nationality.

The example of Brazil or Mexico, where multinational enterprises are very important in terms of volume of investment is revealing in some respects.

Multinational enterprises' share in the manufacturing sector

Country	Total employment (in thousands)	Employment in multinational enterprises (in thousands)	Multinational enterprises' share in employment %	Multinational enterprises' share in sales %
Brazil 1966	1 900	128	6.7	12.0
1970	2 082	176	8.5	18.0
Mexico 1966	1 640	106	6.5	16.0
1970	1 848	184	9.9	25.0

Source: Implications of multinational firms for world trade and investment and US trade and labor, Committee on Finance, US Senate, Washington, DC, 1973.

Thus, at the national level, as already noted for all developing countries taken together, multinational enterprises have a greater share of sales in the manufacturing sector than of employment, their productivity being higher than that of local firms. Similarly, in the industrial sector in Brazil and Mexico, employment in multinational enterprises has grown at a rate well above the average for the sector.

These results are confirmed by another study on Mexico.[1]

Industrial employment in multinational enterprises has grown quickly because their rates of capital accumulation and production growth have risen faster than the productivity of labour. The much smaller growth of employment in national firms is as much due to comparative lack of dynamism as to their rate of modernisation, which is probably higher than in multinational enterprises, for the very reason that until now their capital intensiveness has been so low.

Although multinational enterprises are more dynamic than national ones, they absorb only a small amount of labour. In countries like Brazil or Mexico, where they are well established, they occupy less than 10 per cent of the total force

---

[1] F. Fajnzylber and T.M. Tarrago: Las empresas transnacionales, Mexico City, 1975.

employed in industry.   This, though appreciable in itself, is small in proportion to their share in investment, which is about 30 per cent.   In Panama, where United States-based multinational enterprises are also well to the fore, the number of persons employed by multinational industrial enterprises was 1,989 in 1971, or 4.7 per cent of the total force employed in the manufacturing sector.[1]

<u>Mexico - growth rate of industrial employment</u>
(annual rate - 1965-70)

Branch	Total	Multinational enterprises	National enterprises
Food manufacturing	2.0	13.5	1.2
Beverages	4.8	18.5	3.7
Tobacco	4.3	5.7	2.8
Textiles	-1.7	8.8	-2.0
Clothing	2.8	19.7	2.4
Furniture	12.6	80.0	10.8
Paper	4.0	7.2	3.1
Printing	2.8	12.0	2.3
Leather	2.7	25.0	-2.9
Rubber	4.8	3.0	6.0
Chemicals	5.4	8.1	3.4
Non-ferrous metals	3.5	5.8	3.2
Metals	6.8	2.6	8.3
Metal products	3.1	15.4	2.1
Machinery	5.0	19.0	-0.1
Electrical equipment	6.1	21.0	-4.8
Transport equipment	9.1	12.1	7.1
Miscellaneous	2.3	23.0	-3.2
Total:	<u>3.4</u>	<u>12.1</u>	<u>1.5</u>

This low contribution to employment creation is due first of all to the fact that investment by multinational enterprises increasingly takes the form of buying up firms and less and less of setting up new production units.   This has been pointed out in many studies.   For example, in 1916, 73 per cent of the subsidiaries formed in Mexico by multinational enterprises took the form of new factories. Between 1956 and 1967, the proportion of new production units fell to 34 per cent.[2] Buying up existing firms obviously creates no additional employment.

A second reason why multinational enterprises create relatively little employment in industry is that they invest in industries which are inherently capital intensive and use very advanced techniques.   Various studies have shown that multinational enterprises do not greatly alter the techniques they use in their home country, or in other words that drastic alteration of production techniques to adapt them to the local labour supply position is uncommon.   This point is important enough to deserve more detailed consideration.

With regard to manufactured products, choices of technique, when possible, can be divided into two distinct kinds.   In the first place, one factor of production may be substituted for another in manufacturing any given product.   There is then a

---

[1] Marcos A. Gandásegui: <u>Industrialización e inversiones extranjeras en Panamá,</u> Estudios Sociales Centroamericanos, April 1974.

[2] Fajnsylber and Tarrago, op. cit.

There are several explanations of this situation[1]:

- distortions in the prices of goods and factors leads to increased use of capital;

- markets are too small to encourage a search for solutions appropriate to local market conditions;

- lack of skilled labour leads to capital being substituted for labour;

- the cost of capital is lower for multinational enterprises than for local firms;

- appropriate technologies are relatively limited.

The virtual absence of appropriate technology is a particularly important cause. A study by Chudson concludes that "the material gathered by questionnaire and interviews as well as recently published literature supports the conclusion that in many if not most large-scale manufacturing operations, the opportunity for choosing from among the available technologies a more economically efficient and more labour-intensive technique is extremely limited".[2]

This point is also made in a study on Kenya[3] which points out that in many cases, even when labour-intensive technology exists, it is not used simply because productivity is too low for manufacture to be competitive. For example, a study on tinned food production in Kenya shows that automation is more productive than semi-automatic techniques, but the latter involve extensive use of supervisory staff, whose cost is high.

The problem of the lack of skilled labour is examined at length in several studies.[4] Multinational enterprises sometimes adopt capital-intensive methods for the express purpose of overcoming this problem[5], and when their subsidiaries make alterations in techniques, the result is often to economise the skilled labour which is so scarce in developing countries.[6]

Consequently:

- the fact that the industrial activities in which multinational enterprises invest are inherently capital intensive;

---

[1] R.H. Mason: The transfer of technology and the factor proportion problem: The Philippines and Mexico, UNITAR, 1972; and W.A. Yeoman: Selection of production processes for the manufacturing subsidiaries of US-based multinational corporations, DBA thesis, 1968; Morley and Smith: The choice of technology ..., op. cit.

[2] W.A. Chudson: The international transfer of commercial technology to developing countries, UNITAR, 1971, p. 25.

[3] Employment, incomes and equality: A strategy for increasing productive employment in Kenya, ILO, 1972, p. 451.

[4] Ibid.; R.H. Mason, op. cit.

[5] International Chamber of Commerce: Realities - Multinational enterprises respond on basic issues, 1974.

[6] Cf. also J.H. Dunning: The multinational enterprise, 1971, Chapter 3.

- the relatively stable technology of production processes, and

- the shortage of skilled labour in developing countries,

explain why multinational enterprises create relatively little employment in the manufacturing sector now under consideration. A second conclusion is that employment creation is higher in multinational enterprises than in local firms.

3. Use of cheap labour

The beginnings and quick expansion of investment and international production using labour-intensive processes and relatively unskilled labour appear to date from the 1960s.

There are a number of ways in which it may happen. Broadly speaking, it may vary from assembling components of a product to more complex activities involving processing and manufacturing parts of it. Sometimes subsidiaries are set up to do this, and sometimes it is subcontracted to independent units, either directly by subsidiaries or through agents. Variants are possible with either method, as they are with the mechanics of international subcontracting.[1]

The most usual practice is to set up subsidiaries to assemble components imported from the parent firm and re-export the assembled products to the market of origin. In the United States, this comes under items 806-30 and 807-00 of the tariff schedules covering entry into the United States of goods produced abroad from components exported from the United States, under which import duties are payable only on the value added abroad. Item 807-00 is the one most generally applied (it covers 90 per cent of the total imported under both tariff schedules); item 806-30 applies more particularly to metal producer goods.[2] The United States is not the only country to apply this system; practically all developed countries do so, but make less liberal concessions.

A second, very important relationship between developed and developing countries arises from the trade in certain finished consumer goods such as gloves and toys. According to A. Hone[3] it accounts for recent trends in exports of manufactured products by developing countries.

As the following figures show, investments of this kind by multinational enterprises have expanded rapidly over the last ten years, especially in certain Asian countries:

Direct foreign investments in selected countries of Asia
(in millions of US $)

	1967	1972
Hong Kong	65.0	400.0
South Korea	17.5	300.0
Malaysia	103.0	300.0
Singapore	40.0	150.0
Taiwan	88.0	500.0

Source: 1967, OECD: Stock of private direct investments by DAC countries in developing countries, end 1972, op. cit.; estimates by A. Hone, op. cit., p. 147.

---

[1] Cf. S. Watanabe: "International subcontracting, employment and skill promotion", International Labour Review, May 1972, for forms of subcontracting applicable in international relations.

[2] The most complete study on this theme is to be found in the US Tariff Commission's publication: Economic factors affecting the use of item 807.00 and 806.30 of the tariff schedules of the United States (TC Publication 339, Washington, DC, September 1970).

[3] A. Hone: "Multinational corporations and multinational buying groups: Their impact on the growth of Asia's exports of manufactures - Myths and realities" (World Development, February 1974, pp. 145-149).

The growth rates are extremely high and probably in most of these countries investments have been made in the activities just mentioned.

The very rapid growth of foreign investments, particularly in the assembly of semi-finished products, which is highly labour-intensive, is explained by the presence of cheap labour in the developing countries, rising wages in the developed countries, and the need to remain competitive at home and abroad. The differences in wage levels between the two groups of countries are large enough to justify setting up production units abroad.

As already noted, in this case the multinational enterprise does not change its production technique, but carries out abroad one or more stages of manufacture such as final assembly of the components of a machine, this stage of production being inherently labour intensive. It does so with an eye to export, and this gives an extra benefit to the country in which the investment is made.

Cheap labour is an important element in this strategy.

Average hourly earnings of labour in assembly plants in the United States and developing countries (1970)

	Developing countries (US $)	USA (US $)	Ratio USA/ developing countries
Electronics			
Hong Kong	0.27	3.12	11.8
Mexico	0.53	2.31	4.4
Taiwan	0.14	2.56	18.2
Machine assembly			
Hong Kong	0.30	2.92	9.7
Mexico	0.48	2.97	6.2
South Korea	0.28	2.78	10.1
Singapore	0.29	3.36	11.6
Taiwan	0.38	3.67	9.8
Semi-conductors			
Hong Kong	0.28	2.84	10.3
Jamaica	0.30	2.23	7.4
Mexico	0.61	2.56	4.2
West Indies	0.72	3.33	4.6
South Korea	0.33	3.32	10.2
Singapore	0.29	3.36	11.6
Clothing			
British Honduras	0.28	2.11	7.5
Costa Rica	0.34	2.28	6.7
Honduras	0.45	2.27	5.0
Mexico	0.53	2.29	4.3
Trinidad	0.40	2.49	6.3

Source: C.A. Vaitsos, op. cit.

In practice this advantage in relative wages is profitable not only to US-based multinational enterprises but to all multinational enterprises, including European and Japanese ones. This is shown by the following figures:

Average hourly earnings in assembly plants - 1965 -
Japan and developing Asian countries

	Wage index
Japan	100
South Korea	20
Pakistan	32
India	33
Burma	33
Sri Lanka	36
Thailand	38
South Viet-Nam (Rep.)	41
Philippines	42
Singapore	61

Source: T. Ozawa: Transfer of technology from Japan to developing
countries, op. cit.

These activities of multinational enterprises are inherently labour intensive and their direct employment creation coefficient is high.   The case of Singapore is interesting, for it shows a large-scale influx of foreign investment together with a spectacular rise in industrial employment.

Investment by multinational enterprises and industrial
employment in Singapore

	1965	1967	1969	1971
Investments (in millions of US $)				
Metal products	19	44	78	124
Electronics	1	7	21	107
Chemicals	5	22	30	72
Wood and paper	3	6	33	48
Textiles	7	14	47	52
Food	9	26	31	47
Other products	14	39	95	105
Total all industries:	58	158	335	555
Industrial employment (in thousands)	56.1	71.6	102.9	148.7

Sources: ILO Yearbook of Labour Statistics and W.K. Poh and M. Tan: Singapore
in the international economy, 1972.

The employment figures apply to all establishments and not only to those of multinational enterprises, but the correlation between the enormous growth of foreign investment, which increased ten times between 1965 and 1971, and that of industrial employment is beyond doubt.   The following not very recent statistics give an idea of industrial employment in multinational enterprises.

The contribution of multinational enterprises to direct employment creation is thus very great, averaging 30 per cent in Singapore.   In some sectors, such as textiles and electrical goods, employment creation is still higher in relative value (nearly two-thirds).

Employment in multinational enterprises in Singapore
(December 1968)

Sectors	Multinational enterprises[1]	Total for the sector	Multinational enterprises' percentage
Beverages and food	1 873	9 598	19.5
Textiles	7 190	11 780	61.0
Paper and wood	2 404	9 423	25.5
Rubber and leather	909	2 530	35.9
Chemicals	1 497	3 254	46.0
Petroleum products	586	625	93.7
Non-ferrous metals	673	3 440	19.6
Metals	3 944	18 731	21.1
Electrical equipment	1 522	2 312	65.8
Miscellaneous	1 780	13 140	13.5
Total:	22 378	74 833	29.9 (average)

Source: Adjusted from Asian Development Bank: Southeast Asia's economy in the 1970s, 1971.

[1] These are in reality foreign firms coming under the Pioneer Industries Ordinance of 1959. Most of them are multinational enterprises, but all multinational enterprises did not come under the PIO.

Even though Singapore is an extreme case, there is no doubt that in this respect multinational enterprises' investments in labour-intensive activities in developing countries do much to help those countries' full employment policies. Developing countries therefore compete for this kind of "international subcontracting"[1], but the number of them able to benefit from it is limited, for to be eligible, the host country has to fulfil certain desiderata. Watanabe's information[2] on this point is most instructive: "The Commerce and Industry Department of Hong Kong attributes the active foreign investment there to the following factors:

(a) the dexterity, adaptability and industriousness of the labour force;

(b) a relatively low wage level compared with those in Japan and other developed countries;

(c) minimum government controls and interference with the process of production and business;

(d) advantageous geographical location for marketing;

(e) efficient banking, shipping and other service industries; and

(f) Commonwealth preference granted to Hong Kong products on entry into the United Kingdom and other Commonwealth markets."

To these criteria may be added expenses due to the distance between subsidiaries and parent companies, the term "distance" including bureaucratic restrictions on imports and exports[3], and also the fact that in addition to cheap labour, the host country must offer favourable conditions for foreign investment. Enterprises in

---

[1] M. Sharpston: "International subcontracting", Oxford Economic Papers, 1974; and S. Watanabe: "International subcontracting, employment and skill promotion", International Labour Review, May 1972.

[2] Watanabe, loc. cit., p. 427.

[3] Sharpston, loc. cit., p. 125.

Europe and Japan[1] which were asked for information on this point normally look upon political stability as the main factor in their decisions to invest in developing countries.

Indirect employment effects

Multinational enterprises have indirect employment effects through their inputs, their competition with local firms and the use of the income derived from their activities.

1. Inputs

In spite of the variety of ways in which economic literature treats the concept of indirect employment[2], it is clear that the expansion of a given activity leads to growth of other activities which supply it with inputs: this is merely the result of the inter-industry relations shown by the input-output matrix. This is the type of indirect expansion considered, here.

Inputs may be:

- bought locally, so helping to increase production and local employment; or

- imported; they have then no stimulating effect on the local economy and have an adverse effect on the national trade balance.

There are no macro-economic statistics enabling multinational enterprises to be separated from other firms in an input-output matrix, and all that can be done is to proceed by approximation. Furthermore, there are important differences between the extractive and industrial sectors.

In the extractive industries, sector analysis of typical cases suggests that multinational enterprises have few stimulating effects on the rest of the economy. Their inputs only account for a low percentage of their production, and nearly half of them are generally imported. Admittedly, the other half are of local origin, consisting mainly of energy (motor fuel), transport and public works. The available information tends, however, to show that stimulating effects on production and employment in other sectors of the economy are on the low side.[3]

Indirect employment effects are more important in manufacturing industries in so far as multinational enterprises are better integrated into the local economy. As a result of their high degree of vertical integration and their access to international markets, multinational enterprises have a greater propensity to import than local firms.[4]

In countries where they invest because of cheap labour, multinational enterprises import part of their inputs. An interesting example of this is South Korea, where exporting industries are largely controlled by multinational enterprises and where, on average, inputs of local origin account for only a small part of the total. However, some industries that are well integrated into the local economy buy a very high percentage of their inputs locally.

---

[1] Watanabe, loc. cit., p. 427.

[2] J. Krishnamurty: "Indirect employment effects of investment", in Technology and employment in industry, A.S. Bhalla (ed.), ILO Geneva, 1975.

[3] N. Girvan: Multinational corporations and dependent underdevelopment in mineral exports economies, Yale University, 1972; and I. Ivanov: "International corporations and the Third World", International Affairs, August 1974.

[4] Cf. Fajnsylber and Tarrago, op. cit.; and C. Furtado: Analyse du modèle brésilien, Paris, 1974.

Republic of Korea - proportion of local
inputs to total inputs

Product exported	Proportion of local inputs (per cent)
Raw silk and silk waste	100.0
Cloth	27.9
Finished textile products	7.5
Plywood	3.0
Rubber products	24.5
Chemical fertilizers	63.9
Cement and tiles	82.5
Iron, steel sheeting	4.2
Stainless steel cutlery	11.3
Electronic apparatus	30.7
Average:	21.7

Source: S. Watanabe: "Exports and employment: The case of the Republic of Korea", International Labour Review, December 1972.

Indirect employment creation is probably large in the silk, chemical fertilizer and cement sectors, especially as these largely depend on industries in which labour productivity is low. In other sectors, indirect effects are limited.

The relative importance of indirect effects due to multinational industrial enterprises springs from the practice of subcontracting followed by these enterprises. Commercial subcontracting is usual but industrial subcontracting appears to be less frequent.[1]

Properly organised, industrial subcontracting enables international division of labour and specialisation to be maximised and so gives small firms greater opportunities of participating. Certain Asian and Latin American countries have made it obligatory for foreign multinational enterprises to use a certain proportion of locally manufactured parts and elements[2], but this leads to increased costs[3] which obviously slow down the expansion of industrial subcontracting.

2. Competition by multinational enterprises on the local market

Multinational enterprises have to maintain their positions against their world rivals, and in individual markets they seek to preserve their competitive advantages by diversification.[4] They accordingly have a tendency to set up dominating positions, first in the industries they invest in and then in allied branches, either downstream or upstream.

Mexico provides an example of their search for a strong position in a branch of economic activity and diversification within the country.[5] In 1970, multinational enterprises accounted for about 35 per cent of Mexican industrial production, the breakdown per branch being as follows:

[1] S. Watanabe, "Subcontracting, industrialisation and employment creation", International Labour Review, July-August 1971.

[2] Ibid.

[3] J. Baranson, op. cit.

[4] Cf. G.Y. Bertin: "Multinational growth, oligopoly and competition", in La croissance de la grande firme multinationale, CNRS, Paris, 1973.

[5] Fajnzylber and Tarrago, op. cit.

Sector	Share of multinational enterprises in production (per cent)
Non-durable consumer goods	36
Intermediate products	30
Durable consumer goods	62
Producer goods	36

When strong positions such as this are built up, the least productive enterprises, i.e. some local ones, may be eliminated. Investment in a sector dominated by small local or family enterprises may thus result in some of them being shut down or absorbed, and possibly in a slight fall in employment, or more probably a shift of labour to the multinational enterprises.

Figures already given for Mexico (see p. 8 above) also illustrate the competition by multinational enterprises with local enterprises.

Industrial employment: annual growth rate (1965-1975)

Branch of activity	Multinational enterprises	Local enterprises	Total
Textiles	8.8	-2.0	-1.7
Leather	25.0	-2.9	+2.7
Machinery	19.0	-0.1	+5.0
Electrical goods	21.0	-4.8	+6.1
Miscellaneous	23.0	-3.2	+2.3
All industries	12.1	1.5	+3.4

Very high employment growth rates in multinational enterprises (higher than for the sector as a whole) go together with a fall in employment in local firms. In this example, competition from multinational enterprises has doubtless led to some displacement of manpower from local firms to multinational enterprises. The dynamic expansion of multinational enterprises has not, however, led to a fall in the level of employment except in the textile industry; it has been accompanied by a rise in employment in the branches of activity in question and over industry as a whole.

3. The use of multinational enterprises' income

The use of multinational enterprises' income has an important impact on local employment in so far as these firms reinvest part of their declared profits locally and pay taxes and dues to the government of the host country.

They generally reinvest in the host country a considerable part of their declared profits, which statistics show is particularly high in heavily or moderately industrialised countries and lower in Africa and Asia.

These reinvestments on the spot have beneficial effects on the local economy and so on employment, even though they generally take the form of self-financing and not investment in other branches of activity.

Multinational firms also contribute to the public revenue in host countries. In some countries whose development has not reached an advanced stage, their operations largely determine the scope for financing out of public funds and therefore the employment level.

First, multinational firms pay direct and indirect taxes locally and thereby contribute to the host country's budgetary resources, i.e. to its operating and investment budgets respectively. This encourages employment creation in the public sector and the sectors in which public investments are made. Secondly, they pay levies to the State on the export of their products. This is particularly important in countries where they exploit national resources.

According to Reuber[1], the total amount of taxes levied by developing countries on the operations of American firms was in the region of 3.2 to 4.0 thousand million US dollars in 1970, or about 1 per cent of those countries' gross domestic product. The breakdown of this amount was:

- extractive industries and services: 70 per cent;

- manufacturing industries: 30 per cent, of which American firms paid 15 per cent, i.e. about 600 million US dollars or approximately 32 per cent of their declared profits.

To these figures should be added the amount of taxes paid by non-American firms, which may be roughly estimated at 2-3 thousand million US dollars. Multinational firms therefore had to pay taxes amounting to something like 6-7 thousand million US dollars or about 2 per cent of these countries' gross domestic product; this is an appreciable sum.

Levies paid by multinational firms on exports of their products should also be added. Statistics are not available, but examples suggest that these levies average around 3 per cent of the volume of sales of raw materials (excluding petroleum). Petroleum royalties were 12.5 per cent of the OPEC 1973 posted price. In proportion to multinational companies' total volume of sales, this could represent very roughly 7-10 thousand million US dollars annually, or 2-3 per cent of the developing countries' gross domestic product. This is considerable.

In all, multinational firms may contribute 4-5 per cent of the developing countries' national incomes. This large amount has favourable effects on employment.

---

[1]
   G.L. Reuber, op. cit.

CHAPTER II

THE IMPACT OF MULTINATIONAL ENTERPRISES ON EMPLOYMENT
IN INDUSTRIALISED COUNTRIES

The effect of multinational operations on employment in industrialised countries should be considered from two aspects.

In the first case, industrialised countries encourage foreign undertakings to set up industrial plants on their soil and actively welcome multinational enterprises as a matter of policy. For example, foreign investors are welcome in all countries of Western Europe, and European multinational firms are increasingly establishing themselves in the United States and Canada. In all these cases, the industrialised countries act as host countries.

The second case concerns industrialised countries - sometimes the very ones welcoming investment - which export capital to operate in a foreign country which may be either industrialised or developing. In this event, industrialised countries are considered in their role as home countries.

In the absence of any study of these two aspects by the International Labour Office, the results of a number of analyses have been used.

The industrialised countries as host
countries for foreign investment

From the point of view of employment creation, multinational investments in industrialised countries have aroused little attention. The number of jobs made available by multinational companies in 1970 was however estimated at 13 to 14 million for all market economy countries, and 2 million of these were created in developing countries; it follows that in the industrialised countries, the multinational companies have made a remarkable contribution to employment by creating or maintaining something like 11 to 12 million jobs.[1]

This explains why in the industrialised countries opinions expressed on foreign investment are largely favourable, at least regarding employment. The few reservations made relate to the quality and stability of the employment created.

Examples will be drawn here from a detailed French inquiry into the impact of foreign investment[2], which concludes that it has been good for employment. Setting up new factories, as multinational enterprises have often done, creates much employment. The labour force grows very sharply in the first years, often by more than 10 per cent annually and tends to level off later. When investment is through a takeover of a local firm, employment is at first maintained or occasionally reduced, mainly at executive level, but in the long run the investment leads to increased employment. All in all, foreign takeovers are considered very beneficial, for they have strengthened the firms concerned, especially if they were in difficulties before being taken over. Since national firms were unwilling or unable to absorb them, some businesses would have closed down but for foreign investors.

The new plants set up by foreign investment have also helped industrial diversification. The report mentions operations by Motorola, ITT Cannon and Synelec in the South of France (the Midi - Pyrenees region) and by Tioxide, United Carbide, CGCT, Rifa and Rank Xerox in the North of France.

The report is a little less favourable to multinational enterprises when considering whether the employment they create is as stable as in national enterprises, especially when the trade cycle takes a downward turn. In the case of

---

[1] United Nations: Multinational corporations and world development, op. cit.

[2] Délégation à l'aménagement du territoire et à l'action régionale: Investissements étrangers et aménagement du territoire, Livre blanc, Paris, 1974.

some regions, it does not rule out the possibility that a foreign enterprise
might have less hesitation than a national one in reducing its staff in a serious
slump. In the case of others, it states that no foreign enterprise set up between
1962 and 1971 had ceased operations by the end of 1971, which gives an impression
of stability. Few foreign firms had shut down during the last ten years, but
business then was good. There might be some shedding of labour if it slackened,
but, according to the report, this risk is even more probable in national firms
because foreign enterprises act as shock absorbers during recessions. When
they decide to invest they do so generally on a long-term basis. They often
invest when prospects are bad, taking advantage of the trough in the trade cycle.
They are less affected by recession because they usually belong to expanding
industries and supply the world market, which is not subject to fluctuation in
the same way as national ones. Finally, the scale of their investments makes
for security and their output is generally so specialised and diversified as to
prevent abrupt changes in employment policy.

While in quantitative terms, multinational enterprises appear to make an
essential contribution to employment creation and maintenance, opinions are more
qualified about the degree of skill of the jobs created. It has been found in
some regions that all in all, the quality of employment foreign enterprises offer
is rather limited and sometimes below average for the industry or region. This
depends on the industry and the size of the enterprise; often the work is of
a kind which never employs a high proportion of skilled labour, or the foreign
enterprises may be considerably larger than average for the region. The
report adds that there has recently been an improvement in the level of skill
of jobs in some foreign establishments. This is from within, or at least
is endorsed, by all managements of foreign establishments. Where there are
exceptions, this appears to be because the goods manufactured is such
that the proportion of skilled jobs cannot be increased.

No difference has been observed in the proportion of foreign labour employed
by multinational and national companies. For the higher grades, the situation
was different about ten years ago, but things have changed and the number of
foreign executives is now small; many foreign enterprises have none coming
from the parent company or at most one or two. There are more of them in firms
recently set up, but this is only temporary.

The very favourable assessment expressed in the official report on the impact
of multinational enterprises on employment is tempered by an observation which
seems to indicate that their indirect effects on employment are limited. It
is noted that sometimes these enterprises draw a large proportion of their supplies
from abroad instead of from French contractors and suppliers, and generally
speaking, only a limited volume of work is contracted out to local manufacturers.
There are of course exceptions. The buying policy of firms set up a long while
ago is generally comparable to that of French enterprises, and the plants opened
by some foreign firms, like IBM in Montpellier, have created large numbers of new
jobs in subcontracting and expanded local enterprise. Nevertheless, despite
these exceptions, where foreign firms have set up plants, the local economy has
been mainly called upon to supply services.

The industrialised countries as sources
of foreign investment

Most industrialised countries welcoming foreign investment are themselves
exporters of capital. Thus parent companies with headquarters in the United
States, the United Kingdom, France, the Federal Republic of Germany, the Netherlands,
Belgium, Sweden and Switzerland, for example, have set up plants abroad, either
in industrialised or developing countries.

Seen from this angle multinational investments abroad may have repercussions
on employment levels in the home country. So far, concern about this has been
expressed mainly in the United States, but more recently rising unemployment
has brought the problem to the fore in some Western European countries.

The only detailed studies on the question are those carried out in the
United States as a result of the controversy between the American Federation
of Labor - Congress of Industrial Organizations (AFL-CIO) and the American business

world.[1] As is well known, American multinational enterprises have been attacked by workers' organisations in the United States on the ground that they have adversely affected employment creation, both directly and by reducing American competitiveness abroad. Such studies as have been made come to contradictory conclusions, probably because of differences in the methods used.

The AFL-CIO asserts that the United States position in world trade became much worse during the 1960s, and ascribes this to:

- the enormous growth in American companies' investments abroad, which has led to the internationalisation of technology and reduction of the United States' technical lead, resulting in the export of some jobs to foreign countries;

- the rapid growth in the number of multinational enterprises which have chosen to locate production outside the United States on cost grounds, leading to a considerable fall in American exports.

According to an AFL-CIO investigation made between 1966 and 1969, about 500,000 jobs were lost to the United States in this way. Another investigation by the International Union of Electrical, Radio and Machine Workers shows that between 1966 and the first half of 1971 employment in the United States fell from 169,400 to 131,700 in radio and television receiver manufacture and from 374,200 to 317,700 in the electronics components industry.

The increasingly hostile attitude of most US workers' organisations towards multinational enterprises operating abroad has met with strong opposition from American business. According to the Emergency Committee for American Trade, US multinational enterprises over the last ten years have had a rate of job creation 75 per cent above that of all other industrial enterprises.[2] A study by the US Chamber of Commerce[3] confirms this and shows that multinational enterprises increased their employment in the United States by 31.1 per cent between 1960 and 1970, against an average for the industrial sector of 12.3 per cent. Similarly, a study by R. Stobaugh[4] estimated that American multinational enterprises had created 600,000 jobs in manufacturing industry.

In the absence of any ILO study on the subject, a detailed analysis by R.G. Hawkins[5] has been used. It is interesting mainly as showing that the results[6] are entirely governed by the estimating methods and assumptions adopted. The following summary highlights the uncertain nature of the analyses.

---

[1] Cf. the controversy between the AFL-CIO and multinational enterprises in the United States mentioned in Multinational enterprises and social policy, ILO, 1973; and Senator A.A. Ribicoff's report entitled Implications of multinational firms for world trade and investment and for US trade and labor (12 February 1973). Cf. also the various studies by the US Department of Commerce in 1972, e.g. Policy aspects of foreign investment by US multinational corporations, January 1972.

[2] Emergency Committee for American Trade: The role of multinational corporations in the USA and world economies, Washington, December 1972.

[3] National Foreign Trade Council: The impact of US foreign investment on US employment and trade, New York, 1971.

[4] R. Stobaugh and Associates: US multinational enterprises and the US economy, Harvard Business School, 1971.

[5] R.G. Hawkins: Job displacement and the multinational firm: A methodological review, Center for Multinational Studies, September 1972.

[6] The same conclusions appear in the study made by the Committee on Finance, US Senate, op. cit.

Summary of studies on multinational enterprises'
effects upon employment

Study	Type of analysis or source of information	Net effect on employment
Business International	Sample survey of 86 companies	Positive
Emergency Committee on American Trade	Sample survey of 74 companies	Mainly positive
National Foreign Trade Council	Sample survey and case studies of more than 50 companies	Positive
Ruttenberg, AFL-CIO study	Official data	Negative "to a large extent" (loss of 500,000 jobs)
Stobaugh and Associates	Combination of nine case studies on individual investment decisions with various data	+ 600,000
US Chamber of Commerce	Sample survey of 158 companies	Positive

Source: R.G. Hawkins, op. cit., table I, pp. 5 and 6.

Study	Main conclusions
Business International	Between 1960 and 1970, exports by multinational enterprises increased more rapidly than US exports.
	Between 1960 and 1970, employment in the United States grew more quickly in multinational enterprises (32.8 per cent) than in other sectors (19.5 per cent).
	Multinational enterprises' export surplus grew by $1.7 thousand million between 1960 and 1970.
Emergency Committee on American Trade	From 1960 to 1970, employment in multinational enterprises grew by 3.3 per cent yearly whereas in the United States the average rate for the manufacturing sector was 1.4 per cent.
	Foreign subsidiaries stimulate US exports.
	Multinational enterprises have a sound and growing balance of payments and trade balance.
National Foreign Trade Council	Most foreign investments were made to maintain or extend foreign markets. Foreign investments were necessary to develop exports.
	In most cases American domestic investment was not a valid alternative to foreign investment.

Study (cont.)   Main conclusions (cont.)

Ruttenberg, AFL-CIO study   Multinational enterprises are largely responsible
                                       for deterioration in the American balance of
                                       payments and the "loss" of jobs to the United
                                       States.

                                       Technology transfer by multinational enterprises
                                       harms employment in the United States and the
                                       US trade balance.

Stobaugh and Associates   Multinational enterprises have positive effects
                                       on employment. Foreign investment is made to
                                       preserve existing markets or open new ones, and
                                       has positive effects on the trade balance.

US Chamber of Commerce   Between 1960 and 1970, employment in multinational
                                       enterprises (31.1 per cent) grew more quickly
                                       than total employment in the United States
                                       (12.3 per cent).

                                       Multinational enterprises made foreign investments
                                       mainly to keep markets and overcome trade barriers.

                                       They have a much larger trade surplus than national
                                       firms.

    Comparison of these studies shows clearly that in the present state of
knowledge and on the assumptions adopted it is impossible to say whether American
multinational enterprises have reduced the level of employment in the United
States or not.

    Hawkins' analysis shows that the net effect on employment is the result
of opposing factors.[1] He then attempts a separate estimate of each effect. On
the various assumptions adopted, the net effect on employment (equal to the
aggregate of each separate effect) is between + 279,000 jobs and - 666,000 jobs.[2]
In conclusion: (i) it cannot be asserted that multinational enterprises have
either a positive or negative impact on employment in the United States, and
(ii) employment creation and employment disappearance probably cancel each other
out to some extent.[3]

    In any event, it has to be recognised that growing competition in inter-
national markets often leaves producers no alternative but to export part of
their production facilities. Higher wages in the industrialised countries and
the need to get round the customs barriers of the importing countries reduce
the choices available, so that in any case the number of jobs would have fallen.
Forming foreign subsidiaries is, at least in the long term, likely to create
employment by increasing exports and complementary technical relations with the
parent company, but short-term adjustments will certainly be necessary.

———————

    [1] Op. cit., p. 9, summarises the factors as follows: "Local production
displacement effect; export stimulation effect; home office employment effect;
supporting firm employment effect".

    [2] Ibid., p. 27.

    [3] Ibid., p. 29.

CHAPTER III

THE CONTRIBUTION OF MULTINATIONAL ENTERPRISES TO THE IMPROVEMENT OF KNOWLEDGE IN HOST COUNTRIES

Multinational enterprises may improve knowledge in two ways:

- by technology transfer;

- by training.

Technology transfer

Technology transfer by multinational enterprises may be either through decentralising research and development or through direct investment.

1. Research and development

At first sight, multinational enterprises do little for technology transfer because their research and development are highly centralised.

In the case of the industrialised host countries, the French survey already mentioned[1] shows that nearly all foreign establishments depend entirely on foreign sources for their technology. Research work is mostly carried out in the home country where multinational enterprises often have large research laboratories which do all the fundamental research. There are a few exceptions, such as IBM, Shell and Solvay which have already set up research centres in France, and other foreign countries which are planning research and design centres; this seems to indicate a tendency to decentralise research in future.

In the developing countries there is hardly ever any decentralisation of research[2], and new manufacturing processes are handled centrally by the parent company. Research and development in multinational enterprises is run on the assumption that scientific knowledge is for internal circulation only, so that international dissemination of technology only takes place within the firm.

Of course, multinational enterprises have not a monopoly of research and development in new technology, but they have been most important innovators in computers, pharmaceuticals, plastic products and nuclear energy.[3] Most research and development is in fact done by large firms, the majority of them multinational. In the highly industrialised OECD countries eight firms carry out 30 to 50 per cent of the industrial research and development.[4]

The concentration of research and development in multinational enterprises and its further concentration in the parent companies of these enterprises are accounted for by the economies of scale in research and development, the desire to reduce the technical and commercial risks of experimental work on new products, and the availability of research facilities. This explains why in 1966 only about 6 per cent of total research and development expenditure by American multinational enterprises in the manufacturing sector was done abroad[5]; probably almost none of the 6 per cent was done in subsidiaries in developing countries.

---

[1] Délégation à l'aménagement du territoire et à l'action régionale, op. cit., p. 61.

[2] A.J. Cordell: The multinational firm, Ottawa, December 1971.

[3] K. Pavitt: "The multinational enterprise and the transfer of technology", in The multinational enterprise, J.H. Dunning, op. cit.

[4] OECD: Gaps in technology, Paris, 1968.

[5] United Nations: Multinational corporations and world development, op. cit.

Decentralising research and development by transferring it to developing
countries could however be a very effective means of technology transfer.   There
is plenty of scope for it[1] - in tropical agriculture, more intensive exploitation
of mineral resources, labour-intensive technology and the like, but the small size
of developing countries' markets is a serious handicap.

The answers of a number of American firms questioned on the problem[2] show that
efforts have been made in this direction.   These firms recognise the need to extend
research and development to the developing countries.   The decentralisation they
are aiming at is hampered by political and psychological, rather than technical,
obstacles but the first steps in this direction have given promising results.

2. Direct investment

Among the ways in which developing countries can acquire advanced countries'
technology are the sale of licences, the supply of equipment, and management
contracts[3], but it is clear that non-industrialised countries cannot acquire
innovations without foreign investment by multinational enterprises.

In Ethiopia, the changes since 1955 are due mainly to the import of foreign
technology in the form of machines, intermediate products and equipment ("embodied
technology") and management ("disembodied technology").[4]   The cost of these
transfers was in the region of 3 per cent of the GDP in 1969-70.   The process was
the same in Spain, which also received large-scale technical assistance.[5]

In Chile, most changes up to 1970 showed the decisive influence of the external
sector.   Foreign investment was the main cause of technology transfer, especially
in the industry sector.   Most (75 per cent) of the contracts for technology transfer
were concentrated on four sectors, chemicals, electrical goods, non-electrical and
transport equipment, with the United States accounting for 45 per cent of the
contracts.[6]

It is noteworthy that some contracts for technology transfer contain clauses
requiring the purchasing firms to acquire the greater part of their intermediate
products and capital from the seller or from firms listed by him[7], and often contain
restrictive conditions, especially as regards exports.[8]

---

[1] "Problems in strengthening R and D in LDCs", in National Academy of Sciences:
US international firms and R and D in developing countries (Washington, 1973).

[2] "The role of US firms in strengthening R and D in LDCs", Ibid.

[3] United Nations: The acquisition of technology from multinational corporations by developing countries, New York, 1974.

[4] UNCTAD: Major issues arising from the transfer of technology - a case
study of Ethiopia, Geneva, 1974.

[5] UNCTAD: Major issues arising from the transfer of technology - case study
of Spain, Geneva, 1974.

[6] UNCTAD: Major issues arising from the transfer of technology - a case
study of Chile, Geneva, 1974.

[7] Cf. UNCTAD studies; cf. also J. Carlsen: "The different modes of technology
transfer", Conference on multinational corporations in Africa, IDEP.

[8] UNCTAD: Major issues arising from the transfer of technology - a case study
of Chile, op. cit.

Training by multinational enterprises

Training by multinational enterprises is inseparable from technology transfer. Direct investment consists in transferring equipment and the "know-how" necessary to operate it.   Labour has therefore to be taught the technique involved.

In the case of the industrialised host countries, the French report[1] concludes that foreign multinational enterprises' greatest contribution to local technology is undoubtedly through the training of French executives and specialists in new techniques or comparatively undeveloped branches of activity, and that their contribution in this respect is far from negligible.   They make special efforts to train executives, and often spend more on it than on the training of production operatives, on which their outlay is much the same as for local firms.   When foreign firms spend more, the difference is not due to their nationality but to such factors as their size, modern production processes, and starting-up times.

In the case of the developing countries, the point at issue is the extent to which technology transfers by multinational enterprises raise the level of knowledge in these countries.

The importation of advanced management and production techniques by multinational enterprises may help to improve the skills of local staff in developing countries, but only if the local staff are used in managerial and supervisory posts and in production.   Using them in production obviously raises no problems, but the extent to which they are used in managerial grades should be looked into more closely.

1.   Access of local staff to managerial posts

A major criticism of foreign enterprises concerns the extent to which their local staff take part in management.   It reflects the charge of "extra-territoriality" made by those who feel that foreign companies should be more completely integrated into the host country.

It is hardly possible to generalise on the practice of multinational enterprises in this matter.   It has changed with the passage of time and varies in accordance with several factors.

Local staff of foreign enterprises in developing countries formerly took very little part in management, mainly because there were few executives in those countries, and also because of the attitude of the enterprises, which varied according to their line of business and degree of maturity.

A comparative study of American and European multinational enterprises[2] shows clearly that the proportion of locals and expatriate staff in managerial grades depends on:

- the firm's "degree of internationalisation" - and so, in a sense, of maturity;

- its knowledge of the foreign market;

- the extent to which technology is standardised.

The higher these parameters, the greater the proportion of local staff to expatriates in managerial grades;   in other words, as time goes on, the natural expansion of multinational enterprises appears to make it easier for local staff to reach responsible positions.

---

[1] Délégation à l'aménagement du territoire et à l'action régionale, op. cit.

[2] L.G. Franko: Who manages multinational enterprises?, Centre d'études industrielles, Geneva, 1973.

A study on American multinational enterprises operating in Latin America[1] (which represent the highest degree of maturity of subsidiaries of multinational enterprises in developing countries) shows that from 1966 onwards, they began to employ a very significant proportion of local staff in managerial grades.

Multinational enterprises in Latin America

Breakdown of staff by nationality

1966

Grade	Total		National staff		Expatriate staff		Ratio of national to expatriate staff
	Number	%	Number	%	Number	%	
Managerial and executive	11 693	3.3	10 813	3.0	880	59.4	12 : 1
Technicians	23 044	6.5	22 443	6.3	601	40.6	37 : 1
Other grades	102 353	28.7	102 353	28.8	-	-	-
Workers	219 374	61.5	219 374	61.9	-	-	-
Total	356 464	100.0	354 983	100.0	1 481	100.0	239 : 1

Source: K. May: The effects of United States and other foreign investment in Latin America, Council of Americas, New York, 1971.

But while, over the years, the proportion of local to expatriate staff has increased in multinational enterprises, particularly in industry, the situation is still fluid. In a study involving 81 subsidiaries of multinational enterprises in developing countries[2], three subsidiaries stated that all their executive grades were filled by local staff, and 78 using expatriate staff stressed that they were attempting to increase the ratio of local to expatriate staff to comply with host countries' requirements. These included restrictions on the entry of foreign staff, the submission of proof that local staff could not do the job (e.g. the "Foreign Capital Investment Law" in Indonesia), income tax discrimination, quotas for foreign staff, and compulsory employment of a minimum number of local executives.[3] They reflect government action to increase the part taken by local staff in managing subsidiaries of multinational enterprises. There is still room for improvement, however.

2. Vocational training for production staff

Inquiries covering United States-based multinational enterprises show the importance of training in these firms.[4] In Latin America 63 per cent of the 310 subsidiaries questioned had regular training programmes. These are extremely

---

[1] Quoted by W.A. Chudson, UNITAR, op. cit.

[2] C.G. Howard: "The extent of nativisation of management in overseas affiliates of multinational firms: a world-wide study", Indian Management, January 1971.

[3] Pausenberger, (Verbatim record of the 31st and 32nd sessions of the Federal Parliament of the Federal Republic of Germany, p. 291) quotes as examples Mexico, where 90 per cent of the staff of foreign companies must be of Mexican nationality, the Philippines, where expatriate staff may not exceed 5 per cent of total staff, and Iran, where the employment of foreigners is subject to the grant of a permit for a period generally limited to six months.

[4] L. Weintraub: International manpower development - a role of private enterprise in foreign assistance, New York, 1969.

varied, range from marketing to executive training, and include industrial paint-
ing and courses in reading.

Another study covering eight multinational enterprises[1] in the chemical,
electrical, petroleum, rubber goods and transport equipment industries brings out
the following facts.   All the enterprises stress the lack of well-trained executives.   Whilst admitting that it is possible to train uneducated manpower for
work in industry, they point out that it is expensive and difficult.   Training is
easiest for semi-skilled labour.   Over and above training problems in the strict
sense of the word, there is the difficulty of inculcating the habit of working in
a given environment, and in practice this kind of apprenticeship is arduous.
Training is given at all levels of skill - operatives, office workers and executives.
Executive training receives special attention and takes place both in the subsidiary
and in periods spent with the parent company.

Another study made in the Philippines and Mexico[2] leads to the two broad
conclusions that in these countries there is no fundamental difference between
multinational enterprises and local firms regarding training, and that conditions
vary widely from one company to another.

The OECD[3] has carried out an inquiry on skill development, in the course of
which it approached 48 multinational enterprises based on Western Europe, Japan
and the United States and active in various sectors of industry.   It came to the
conclusion that they devote considerable attention to training, and proportionately
more to vocational and technical training than to executive training.   A survey
by the International Organisation of Employers reached similar conclusions.[4]

3.   Other contributions by multinational enterprises

Training their own staff enables multinational enterprises to remain competitive on local and world markets, but they are often obliged to extend training
beyond their immediate interests.   Many of them have had to recognise that to sell
equipment is not enough, and they must also provide maintenance services and train
customers and their staffs.   Such training has become very widespread in some
enterprises, particularly in developing countries, and it is becoming increasingly
common for sales contracts to include training clauses.

When multinational enterprises resort to subcontracting in developing countries,
another form of training is often provided in the form of help to local businessmen
in organising their production and training their employees.   It proves an effective way of ensuring that supplies are of the requisite quality, and of helping to
improve labour skills in local industry.

There are plenty of examples to show that subsidiaries of multinational
enterprises work closely with national training institutions in host countries and
do much to make the national system more efficient.   Their co-operation is
especially beneficial to developing countries, where it often leads to the use of
the most modern methods of vocational training and more particularly to the intro-
duction of systematic apprenticeship.

---

[1] R.B. Helfgott: "Multinational corporations and manpower utilisation in
developing nations", The Journal of Developing Areas, January 1972.

[2] R. Hal Mason, op. cit.

[3] E. Moll: "Technical assistance and private enterprise", OECD Observer,
No. 31, December 1967, p. 35.

[4] IOE: Multinational enterprises, the reality of their social policies and
practices.

Co-operation between multinational firms and local institutions may take various forms, such as membership of training or examining boards, the establishment of training standards, the supply of free training material and the provision of instructors.

Subsidiaries of multinational enterprises opening up in developing countries generally have to cope with a standard of education inadequate for work in modern industry.   Since much of the labour they have to train is illiterate and of rural origin, they run literacy courses for workers and their families.   Without doubt, such measures help to raise the educational standard of the local community.

_____

CHAPTER IV

SUMMARY

    This essay has confined itself to asking a number of questions on a little-
known subject, namely how multinational enterprises influence employment in host
and home countries and help to improve knowledge in host countries.

    Incomplete and limited though it is, the foregoing analysis enables a number
of provisional conclusions to be drawn.   These are summarised hereafter.

Direct and indirect effects on employment in host countries

    The number of jobs made available by multinational enterprises has been
estimated at 13 or 14 million for all countries in which they operate.   About
74 per cent of their foreign investment has been made in developed countries and
only 26 per cent in developing countries;   it is not surprising therefore that of
the total number of jobs made available by multinational enterprises, 12 million
have been created in the developed countries and 2 million in the developing
countries.

    It is generally accepted that multinational enterprises' investments have
benefited employment in the industrialised host countries.   Their main contribution has undoubtedly been the creation of jobs by opening new plants.   When they
take over a local firm, often one in difficulties, they sometimes reduce staff,
especially at executive level, but altogether their operations are considered
beneficial because they rescue firms which would have closed down but for a foreign
investor.   In the long run the takeovers will mean increased employment.   In a
recession, multinational firms may to some extent act as shock absorbers, since the
employment they create is at least as stable as that created by local enterprises.

    Multinational enterprises' employment record is less favourable when the
indirect effects of their operations in industrialised host countries are examined.
It appears that their supplies are not drawn from local sources to the extent that
might be wished, and also they do not subcontract work to local firms to more than
a limited extent.   Admittedly services, in particular local transport contractors,
have derived benefit from the presence of multinational enterprises, but a change
in supply and subcontracting practices might have a better indirect effect on
employment in industrialised host countries.

    Employment creation by multinational enterprises in developing countries is in
the region of 2 million.   In itself this may appear a very substantial figure, but
its effects seem slight when compared with the total labour force in the Third
Workd, which has benefited by it only to the extent of 0.3 per cent.   If it is
compared with the number of unemployed, however, multinational enterprises may be
said to have achieved appreciable results.

    An over-all, macro-economic estimate is, however, meaningless, for multi-
national enterprises do not operate in all the Third World countries but are
geographically concentrated in some of them, and limit their operations to certain
branches of the economy.   Also, they are usually active in the modern sector of
industry, which, whether multinational or national, does not lead to large-scale
employment creation.

    Sector-by-sector analysis of industry shows that their employment effects are
quantitatively small in the extractive industries.   In this inherently capital-
intensive sector, individual enterprises are not entirely free to choose their
technology.   The limited contribution to employment made by multinational mining
and petroleum industries is due to production conditions in this sector.

    Multinational enterprises have a much higher rate of employment creation in
manufacturing.   They have made an essential contribution to employment in
developing countries, although in absolute terms their employment creation has not
been large enough to be decisive.   If the subsidiaries that were able to do so
relied more on labour-intensive techniques, employment creation would be still
higher.   It should, however, be borne in mind that there is often very little
scope for altering production techniques, which are dictated by the size of the

market and above all by the type of product. Although some industries may not have lived up to expectations, this is not because of the nationality of the enterprises but because of the kind of products they manufacture. Consequently, more employment would not be created by producing any product by labour-intensive techniques; the important thing is to manufacture products which have an inherently high labour content. In such circumstances it is for governments to exercise a choice by encouraging the manufacture of one product rather than another.

Many multinational enterprises have transferred their production, or the part of it with a high labour content, to subsidiaries abroad because of the lower wages paid in the Third World. Such operations are often called "international subcontracting" and do much for employment creation in developing countries, but there seem to be only a limited number of countries able to benefit from future production transfers of this kind.

The indirect employment effects (on employment in other branches of activity) of multinational enterprises in developing countries obviously vary from one sector or country to another. Generally speaking, enterprises in the extractive industries make very little contribution to employment in other sectors. The indirect effects are greater in manufacturing because of subcontracting by multinational enterprises, which gives a stimulus to the rest of the economy so that indirect employment grows perceptibly.

This favourable estimate of multinational enterprises' activity in the manufacturing industries is slightly tempered by the fact that they can of course sometimes compete with local firms and drive them out of business. The effect on employment will usually be negligible, but labour will be displaced towards the multinational enterprises.

Effect on employment in the home country

Research into the impact of multinational enterprises in their home countries does not make it possible to assert with confidence that investments abroad reduce employment in the home country. Some studies say they do, others deny it; everything depends on the basic assumptions. A recent critical survey in the United States on the research carried out there concludes that the net effect of investments abroad on employment in the United States may vary from + 279,000 to - 660,000 jobs, depending on the basic assumptions.

The International Labour Office has not made a detailed study of the subject and so has not come to any valid conclusion. All that can be said is that investments abroad may cause and accelerate structural change in the home country requiring appropriate short-term adjustments.

The improvement of knowledge by multinational enterprises

Knowledge in developing countries may be improved by technology transfer and by training management staff and production workers.

Multinational enterprises can of course act as intermediaries whereby advanced technology is passed on to the Third World, but as a general rule, progress on these lines is still very limited. Research and development are still highly centralised and are usually done in the home country of the capital involved. There is slow progress as multinational enterprises evolve.

Training executive staff in new techniques is unquestionably a greater contribution with regard to technology. Improving skills in developing countries keep pace with the extent to which local executive staff are promoted to managerial posts in local subsidiaries. The general tendency in multinational enterprises is to replace expatriate staff as soon as this can be done without prejudice to efficiency. This is a step in the right direction and has produced excellent results.

In the industrialised countries, there is little difference between vocational training programmes in multinational and local enterprises. Situations vary greatly, but all in all it cannot be said that the average multinational enterprise behaves differently from other enterprises in this respect.

In developing countries, vocational training by multinational firms compares very favourably with that normally available locally. The close co-operation with host country institutions which has often become the rule has no small influence on national vocational training systems.

choice of technique in the strict sense of the term, and it entails a cost which is
not necessarily offset by the profits made from local factors of production.   In
the second place, choices of technique may depend merely on fragmenting the production process.   Manufacture of a product is not a homogeneous process, but is made
up of different stages each involving a more or less labour-intensive technique.
Instead of manufacturing an entire product abroad, multinational enterprises can
therefore confine themselves to carrying out abroad only certain stages of its production or even only one stage, such as final assembly;   assembling tractors in
developing countries is a good example of this.   There is then, strictly speaking,
no choice of technique, but merely a choice of product.   This second kind of choice
of technique is completely distinct from the first and will be dealt with later in
this chapter when the use of cheap labour is considered.   For the moment, the point
at issue is choice of technique in the strict sense of the term.

Generally speaking subsidiaries of multinational enterprises in developing
countries make hardly any alteration in the production techniques used in the parent
company.

There are, of course, cases in which there is a shift towards labour-intensive
techniques.   For example, a Japanese glass manufacturing company has set up a subsidiary in India half the size of the parent company and employing three times as
many workers.   Cutting is done by hand and transport of primary products is not
automated.[1]   Other studies show that minor changes in production techniques are
sometimes made, more especially when the product itself is altered.[2]

Another study on Brazil[3], shows that United States-based multinational enterprises working in Brazil use production processes appreciably different from those
used in the United States.   The capital-labour ratio is three to four times lower,
according to the branch of activity, in Brazilian subsidiaries than in the United
States, and the value added per worker is half as much.   Interviews and inventories
of material confirm that Brazilian subsidiaries use much less automatic equipment
than comparable parent companies in the United States.   They also tend to substitute
labour for capital in certain peripheral parts of the production process.   This
does not mean that multinational enterprises have adapted themselves to Brazilian
market - particularly labour market - conditions in the best possible way;   other
analyses[4] show that they do not go far in seeking alterations.   Also, production
techniques are altered because of the size of the market and the quality of the
product (which is lower than in the United States), not because labour is more
plentiful and cheaper in Brazil than in the United States.

An inquiry carried out in 78 multinational enterprises[5] of different nation-
alities and in different host countries reveals that 57 of them had not made any
alteration in the production techniques they imported.   Where technology had been
adapted, it was for reasons connected with the size of the market and the quality
of the products.   These results are interesting, for they confirm those given by
the study on Brazil.

---

[1]
T. Ozawa: Transfer of technology from Japan to developing countries, UNITAR,
1971.

[2]
J. Baranson: International transfer of automotive technology in developing
countries, UNITAR, 1971.

[3]
S.A. Morley and G.W. Smith: The choice of technology: Multinational firms
in Brazil, mimeographed, January 1975.

[4]
S.A. Morley and G.W. Smith: Managerial discretion and the choice of technology by multinational firms in Brazil, Rice University, Houston, Texas, 1974.

[5]
G.L. Reuber: Private foreign investment in development, Oxford University
Press, 1973.